As someone those of my attraction to read about the most popular song of all time was very strong. I have enjoyed reading this so much and the personal stories made the book for me. Stories are how we best learn and remember - and these stories were perfect. There is also so much joy here and it's good to associate this psalm with joy and not, as we often do, with the dirge-like version we have heard at so many funerals. Great songs hold great truths and in this beautiful short reflection on the Twenty Third Psalm, Murray Watts strips away years of our over-familiarity with the poem to reveal a true story of divine love.

Ricky Ross
Singer-songwriter, founding member and lead singer of Deacon Blue

Absolutely brilliant! This book shows us how to live life to the full, under the loving care and guidance of the Shepherd. If we follow the advice revealed in this psalm, wisely explained by Murray Watts, our lives will be transformed. Welcome Home!

Fiona Castle OBE
President, Activate Your Life

MURRAY WATTS

FOR LIFE

The Beauty and Wonder of Psalm 23

Published 2021 by Waverley Abbey Resources, a trading name of CWR,
Waverley Abbey House, Waverley Lane, Farnham, Surrey GU9 8EP, UK.
Registered Charity No. 294387. Registered limited company No. 1990308.
For a list of National Distributors, visit waverleyabbeyresources.org/distributors

Quotes from Henri Nouwen on pages 117 and 120 are from:
Cross Currents Interviews, Brian C Stiller   Vision TV

Every effort has been made to ensure that this book contains the correct
permissions and references, but if anything has been inadvertently overlooked,
the Publisher will be pleased to make the necessary arrangements at the first
opportunity. Please contact the Publisher directly.
Concept development and editing by Waverley Abbey Resources.
Design and production by Waverley Abbey Resources.
Printed in the UK by Page Bros.
ISBN: 978-1-78951-271-7

In memory of my grandfather
Arthur Watts (1871 – 1959)
Founder of Kingsmead School, Hoylake

Thank you for singing this song
with your whole life

And for my grandchildren, Audrey (7),
Ronan (4) and Micah Watts (3 months)
in the hope that you will grow up
to sing this song too

Murray Watts

Murray Watts is an award-winning playwright who has written for theatre, radio, TV and film. He studied English Literature and the History of Art at Emmanuel College, Cambridge and he was one of the founding directors of Riding Lights Theatre Company in York. He is best known as the screenwriter of the internationally acclaimed movie *The Miracle Maker*. He has written many books, including the best-selling *Lion Bible for Children* which has been translated into more than 20 languages. He continues to write plays, screenplays and inspirational books. Twenty-five years ago he moved to Scotland, where he founded *The Wayfarer Trust*, an arts charity based at Freswick Castle in Caithness, which provides encouragement and spiritual inspiration to many people in the world of arts and media.

Contents

The most beautiful song in the world

This is a stupendous claim to make for any song. Perhaps it is absurd because we no longer have the original music for this song, although it has been set to music in a thousand different ways.

We all have our favourite songs and we could survey the world and come up with a top 100, and then a top 20 and, finally (in the way beloved of TV channels wanting to create a whole evening of cheap entertainment), we could come up with a public vote and agree on 'the most beautiful song in the world'.

My guess is that our vote, even if it was truly a global result, would come up with the most 'popular', the most 'romantic', the most 'commercially successful' or the most 'fashionable' song.

But would anyone be listening to this ultimate Number One song in 3000 years' time? Perhaps. But would listening to it, or just reading the words alone, fill your life with beauty and courage, and change the whole way you see the world?

Would one brief song, however popular, give you the strength and inspiration to endure wars and pandemics and all the chaos and trouble and fear that life can bring?

In my view, the twenty-third psalm will never be knocked off the Number One position.

Prologue

This song is 3,000 years old. It was written by a shepherd who became a king. It is very short but in little over 100 words it will take you on a journey which can change the way you see the world. The beauty of these words will invade your soul and, although the original music is long forgotten, a hidden music will rise up within you and fill your life with joy. You will understand why it is truly the most beautiful song in the world.

You can read this song in less than a minute. You can read this book in less than two hours. But if you are serious about a new start, a new kind of living and loving, you must continually travel on this journey. You need to learn this, the most beautiful of all songs, by heart and sing it from the deepest place in your being and, like any great artist, commit to the years of practice such glorious music requires.

Perhaps you didn't know you were a 'great artist'? In the spiritual realm, you can be. In the same sense, you can be a great scientist too, endlessly curious, open-minded, ready to adjust your theories if you are presented with new and compelling evidence.

Great artists and scientists alike need a childlike spirit of adventure, they must be ready to go beyond their own preconceptions and the prejudices of others and the fashionable ideas of the day. They must remain open. So must you, when everything conspires to distract and divert you from this song. Inner and outer voices will tell you that it is irrelevant to your life, when the exact opposite is true. It may well be that there is nothing more important for you now.

If your heart is open to love, then this song is for you. It is not about romantic love but it will bring far deeper love into all your relationships.

If you have no interest in religion but consider yourself spiritual, then this song is for you. You may substitute the word 'Love' for 'Lord' and recognise, however simply, that there is something bigger than yourself at work in the world. Recognising a 'Higher Power', even in a very vague sense, is often the beginning of the greatest journey of transformation.

If your life is in deep trouble, then this song is for you. More than any other song or poem, it has been read in desperate times and brought comfort to the broken-hearted and the dying.

If your life is successful, happy and fulfilled, then this song is for you. For why wouldn't you want to go deeper and further into a peace and happiness that is beyond your wildest dreams?

No one has ever written a more hopeful and more enduring and more beautiful song than this. It's time to take the first step on the journey.

THE LORD

IS MY

Shepherd

'Is the universe a friendly place?'

According to Einstein, this is the greatest question facing humanity.

We have many reasons to answer 'No'. We can gaze at the stars and feel blessed to be alive beneath such beauty, but we are gazing at colossal furnaces which have unimaginable powers of destruction.

In the far reaches of space, there are black holes which can collide and destroy whole galaxies.

We can celebrate the glories of the animal kingdom on earth but we can also wonder whether a giant meteor will destroy us all, just like the dinosaurs were obliterated 65 million years ago.

Our earthly home seems fragile, even without such 'Doomsday' scenarios. There are terrible natural disasters as tectonic plates slide over each other, creating earthquakes and tsunamis. There are volcanoes, hurricanes, floods, fires... There are random forces that can kill hundreds of thousands of people and make millions homeless.

And, perhaps worst of all, human greed, violence and evil have led humanity to the brink of self-destruction and, despite the horrors of two world wars, men, women and children are still being slaughtered on an industrial scale.

In our time, the COVID-19 pandemic has swept the world, blindly killing huge numbers of people in many nations. No doubt there will there be more viruses to come, bringing new challenges for the human race.

There is very little that is 'friendly' about life on earth or throughout the entire universe. And there is no shortage of scientists, intellectuals, artists and philosophers who point out that blind forces, chance, ruthless competition for food and territory, survival of the fittest and the whole process of the evolution of life itself is beyond all morality, all human concepts like 'friendly' or 'hostile'. This is the way things are.

We are born into an impersonal universe. We live short lives full of conflict and suffering. We may get lucky for a while, experiencing some love, happiness, friendship and joy, but we have no right to expect anything good from the universe and eventually all our hopes and dreams will end in oblivion.

I am writing this short book because I believe that this way of seeing the universe, although very understandable and now commonplace, is a more powerful myth than any religion – and it is very seductive.

According to Psalm 23, the universe *is* a friendly place. No matter what we experience, we are told that 'The Lord is my shepherd.'

Who is 'the Lord'? He is the Creator of the

Universe and His character determines the nature of the universe, the essential truth at the core of its very existence.

What is that truth? It is love.

Elsewhere in the Bible we are told, 'God is love' and all understanding of God, and His universe, must come back to this astonishing truth. Love is at the heart of everything.

It is why you exist.

It is why you long for love. It is why you cry out for love, feel wounded when you are abandoned by parents, lovers, friends, children. It is why you are so deeply moved by great love stories. It is why you long for the world to be more like the great stories, the great movies, the great poems, paintings and songs that sing of love.

Love is why you are. And love is at the heart of the whole universe.

'The Lord is my shepherd'. Love will guide you.

This is a promise and because it is a promise made by God Himself, in a thousand different forms in the Bible, it cannot be broken.

It is a truth which has been proved in millions of lives over 30 centuries, since a young shepherd first dreamed up these beautiful words.

Love is your guide. The eternal principle of love. Love is not an impersonal force. It does not act randomly; there is no chance involved. It is personal. It is eternal. It is the very character of God Himself and any religion, or tradition, whether Jewish or Christian or Muslim or any other, which loses sight of love as the very core of our existence and our identity, is losing sight of God Himself. For rules, commandments, traditions, rituals, sermons and hymns will do no good at all if they are not ways of conveying this greatest of all truths to the world: 'God is love'.

That love should be the Lord of your life. That love will be your guide, your shepherd; no matter what happens, nothing can separate you from such love.

My grandfather, who was a Victorian gentleman, was full of stories about the love of God, and sadly his kind of piety and integrity are rare today. His beliefs and his so-called Victorian values are the subject of mockery and disdain in many areas of modern society. But I have always remembered a story he told me about a little shepherd boy who was taught at Sunday School to recite these five words counting them on each finger: 'The – Lord – is – my – Shepherd.' He was encouraged to hold his fourth finger on the word 'my', to show that this is the most intimate truth of all. He is 'my' shepherd. Until we are able to hold the fourth finger firmly and say 'my' we will not know the power of these words for ourselves.

The little shepherd boy had a special love of Psalm 23, because he understood the lives of sheep and how they would wander off and need rescuing on so many occasions. But one winter, searching for sheep stranded in the snow, the little shepherd boy went missing. He was discovered, eventually, frozen in a snow drift, with his hand holding his fourth finger: 'The Lord is *my* shepherd.'

At first glance, this might seem a sentimental story, typical of the period, but when I heard it more than sixty years ago it struck me even then that death could not separate the boy from the love of God. This was a story with an unhappy ending and yet somehow love was far stronger than death.

My grandfather had founded a school in 1904 and the boys were like his own children. During the First World War, he was heartbroken to see about 15 of his beloved school children slaughtered on the Western Front. He had taught all those boys to know 'The Lord is my shepherd' and that 'Love is stronger than death'.

At the time of writing, my grandfather's school, which has survived 116 years of wars, recessions and crisis, has been forced to close permanently. COVID-19 has played its fatal part among many challenges. There is an atmosphere of fearful uncertainty around many schools, charities, businesses and brave enterprises. But love is still stronger than death. It is no surprise that the Queen, a Head of State who believes deeply in a loving God, delivered this message on the 75th anniversary of VE Day to a nation in lockdown: 'Our streets are not empty; they are filled with the love and the care that we have for each other.'

Love is at the heart of the universe, not war or pandemics.

The Lord is my shepherd and He will go first, in the way of Middle Eastern shepherds. He always goes first, calling the sheep to follow. He goes through our lives, ahead of us. He will also be ahead of us, even when we die. There is nowhere He will not guide us

If the song we sing with our lives is 'the Lord is my shepherd', there is nothing we cannot do or become, because gradually we will take on some of the character of God Himself.

Love will be in our hearts and we will be drawn ever closer to the Centre of the universe.

I SHALL

NOT

We don't use the word 'want' like this anymore, although there are still echoes of the old form in our language. We use the phrase 'he was found wanting', meaning lacking or insufficient or inadequate. We might still say 'you will want for nothing' meaning 'you will have everything you need.' But today the word 'want' has a bold and blunt meaning. 'I want that.' 'This is what I want.' 'I want a drink.' 'I want a pay rise.'

We hear the word on the lips of little children, 'I want!' 'I want an ice cream!' 'I want that Barbie doll!!'

You could say that our whole society is screaming out, 'I want!' We understand the difference between 'wants' and 'needs' and there is no doubt that our needs are far fewer than our wants, but the spirit of the age is acquisitive, even when it comes to love and sex. Increasingly, we bring a sense of entitlement to all our thinking. 'I have my rights and I want what's mine.'

This is why the ambiguity of the old use of the word is still so powerful: 'I shall not want' ('I shall not keep saying, 'I want!') because I will want for nothing (I will have everything necessary for a good life).

'I shall not want' because the Creator of the universe gives me life and breath, food and clothing, friendship and love.

The Lord is my shepherd and He will guide me into the best possibilities for my life. To believe this, is to live a life liberated from all greed, from the stupidity and blindness of a selfish and narcissistic culture which continually shouts, 'I want!'

So deep is the power of this thought, of this new life, that we will become concerned with what others want. It will matter to us that there are people without clothes or food or medicines or friendship or love and, increasingly, we will become ambassadors in every small and every large way we can. Why? It is because the Lord is my shepherd and He gives me everything I need for a good and purposeful life. I do not need to waste energy or negative emotion, envy, resentment, covetousness, considering all the things I do not have, all the things I endlessly 'want'. Instead, peace will flood my soul, and gratitude, at the simplest kind of provision.

Sunlight on my cheek, five minutes to sit in silence on a park bench in a crowded city, the reassuring word of a friend, a hot cup of tea held in my hand, a warm bath at the end of a fraught day, a cloud of starlings filling the blue sky with endless shapes, shifting and changing and disappearing, a gift from nature.

Perhaps too much is made of 'mindfulness' now, as if it were some wonderful Twenty-First Century discovery, but its roots are in the ancient world. It is because we have forgotten how to pray, how to live, how to follow the goodness of God in the simplest pathways of our experience, that we need to recover 'mindfulness'. But we should not spend our lives being mindful only of ourselves. We need to be mindful of where we come from, who we are, our vulnerability like wandering sheep in the wilderness of our modern world, but above all we need to be mindful of our Shepherd, to follow our Shepherd, away from wanting so much from life and towards celebrating what we already have. Our minds need to be transformed so they are completely in tune with the Shepherd, so we can hear His loving call, drawing us away from self-obsession towards a world that needs our healing power.

But first we must be healed ourselves.

The beginning of Psalm 23 calls us to a place of healing that will change us forever.

Will we allow this to happen?
Will we say, 'The Lord is my shepherd, I shall not want'?

HE MAKES

ME TO

Lie down

IN GREEN

PASTURES

It is extremely difficult to make sheep lie down. You can lead them to a field but you cannot make them lie down.

Sheep will lie down only when they feel safe.

You cannot order sheep to 'lie down'; you can only make them feel safe.

If you ask anyone, 'What do children need most?', the chances are they will reply, 'Love'. Yet what millions of children throughout the world need more than anything, even more than 'love', is safety.

There are countless children whose parents love them but who do not feel safe. In many cases, it is because they are living through the nightmare of a war zone. This is the tragic reality of Twenty-First Century life in Syria, Iraq, Libya and Afghanistan.

But it is also the reality for children who live in families that are plunged into a domestic war zone. They may receive plenty of verbal reassurance from mothers or fathers that they are loved, but they are not safe.

A child growing up in a home where a mother is obsessed with tidiness, who is frequently on the receiving end of her rage and unhappiness, may hear a great deal about how much she is loved, but she will live in fear. She is not safe.

A child whose father drinks heavily and lashes out blindly, or who is given to fits of irrational anger, or who abandons the home for periods of time, or who leaves forever, may treasure presents and cards that offer a few memories of love, but he will not be safe.

He will not be safe in his father's love.

When a person feels unsafe, no matter what is said to them, the deepest emotional truth will always be that they feel unloved.

Unpredictable parents, who swing from exaggerated declarations of love to rage, accusation, disappointment and then back to regret and cuddles and presents and love, create children who feel unstable, unsafe and without protection in an unpredictable world.

War zones, whether the horrific reality of violence and bloodshed and random destruction, or the hidden battlefields of dysfunctional and broken families, fill the world with wounded souls.

Are you wandering, lost in the aftermath of a battle, still trying to find your way in a frightening and unsafe world?

'The Lord is my shepherd, I shall not want, he makes me to lie down…'

He creates a safe space for me, a space that I have never known before. The space of true loving, of a consistent, caring, unchanging, indestructible loving.

The one who created space itself, the unimaginable reaches of the cosmos, space that we cannot comprehend, can create a special space for your heart and your life.

A safe space.

As you slowly enter this space, you will see that all around is goodness and love. You will see that this is the essential truth at the heart of the universe.

The universe is not only a friendly place; it is friendly towards you. Because God made you and loves you far more than any parent or any lover. And God has chosen to reveal Himself to you at last in silence and in safety.

Look around and you will see that there are green pastures. There are fields and streams and trees and flowers bending in the breeze. This is one of the many landscapes of your soul, but the Shepherd wants to lead you here first, so you can discover that peace and safety are the first principles of your life.

You cannot live a glorious life, or fulfil your destiny, if you do not come here first and experience the great peace at the heart of the universe. If you do not lie down in safety. If you do not see that God is for you. He is not against you. He is on your side. He loves you. His love is infinite, personal, particular. He cares about every detail in your whole life.

But, for now, He just wants you to rest for a while in His presence. In green pastures, in a place which is truly fertile and where hope can grow again.

He leads you into a healing place so that one day you can help to bring healing to His world. But, for now, He says, 'Rest'. All His attention is on you. All His healing is for you.

HE LEADS

ME BESIDE

THE

Still

waters

I live beside the sea. As I write, I am looking out over gentle waves tumbling on the shore, but this sea can become wild and dangerous. A few miles from here, the North Sea meets the Atlantic Ocean in the narrow straits called the Pentland Firth, and this is one of the most notoriously treacherous shipping routes in the world.

Every year people are drowned. A few years ago, 12 Polish sailors were lost in a terrible storm. There is an old wreck beneath the calm bay here, and another tilting on the sands off the island of Stroma. This coastline is a graveyard for lost dreams, ventures that came to nothing, lives cut short, the hopeless battle of humanity against the elements. Even the great cliffs and the endless sand dunes are being slowly eaten by coastal erosion.

What would rising sea levels do here? When the storms come in the winter, when the whole sea turns white with fury, I am reminded of the devastating forces at work in the world. Three years ago, I had trees blown down, a wall destroyed, half a roof ripped off in winds of more than 100 miles an hour. But this is nothing compared to the extreme weather events that seem to multiply each year, the impact of climate change in floods and fires, storm, destruction, drought and worldwide devastation. The prophets of doom point to corporate greed, conspiracy, political inertia and what seems to be some kind of suicidal streak in the psyche of the human race. 'Let's deal with this tomorrow' is just as fatal as 'Let's deny this is happening'. Both are a form of slow-motion suicide.

Wild elements, hostile forces of nature, pandemics, raging winds and turbulent seas…

There is no sign of 'still waters' anywhere. There is no stillness in the human heart. Two hundred years ago, William Wordsworth stood on Westminster Bridge in London and wrote: 'Getting and spending, we lay waste our powers'.

If there was still water anywhere, would we look for it?

Some say that the 'still waters' in Psalm 23 refer to wells and watering places in the desert, the kind of water you would long to find in an oasis after a journey through a barren landscape.

'He leads me beside the still waters.' It's a beautiful phrase and there is a whole poem in this.

Still waters are hard to find. Everywhere I look, where I live, I can see the roaring burn carrying melted snows into the sea. I can watch the waves hurl themselves at the cliffs and the white spray showering the dark rocks that appear and disappear with the tides. I am constantly watching one of nature's 'action movies'…

But when the water is very calm, like a mirror, perhaps for a few days in June when the sun hardly sets and the light seems so pure and clear across the ribbed sand and the rock pools, there is a miraculous gift of stillness.

A few days and nights, when I walk alone on the beach. 'He leads me beside the still waters.'

All I can hear are the lapwings, the kittiwakes, the curlews and the very faint sound of water lapping.

But somewhere here is an ancient well, which I have not found. This was the source of pure water, centuries ago.

Water from beneath the earth, fresh water.

A place of life. Because the sea can be pitiless, as the Ancient Mariner observes; 'Water, water, everywhere, nor any drop to drink'.

Fascination, furious energy, street life, city life, the hectic, crazy rhythm of commuting and cars and trains… 'Water, water, everywhere, nor any drop to drink'.

'He leads me beside the still waters.' In this world of violent upheavals, of unpredictable tides and winds and water levels, of drought and fire and disaster, He leads me to a deep well, forgotten, long-hidden.

He leads me to the one place where there is still water, because I must drink for the journey that lies ahead.

We look with fascination and dread at sci-fi films depicting the pitiless world of Mars, which lost its oceans millions of years ago. We imagine what it would be like to discover water there, or create rivers, but we do not see that the spiritual waters of our own world are in danger of drying up. We do not realise that we ourselves are victims of a deadly kind of drought. Our souls are on fire with thirst.

'He leads me beside the still waters.'

He will lead me to where I can drink at last, and keep drinking. He leads me to a place, which I have forgotten, or never known, where I can discover His love, and the knowledge of this love will be pulled up from far below, from deep down in the earth, from the hidden resources of the universe itself. Living water, fresh water, a completely new kind of water, the water of life itself, will be given to me.

At the very moment when the news is bad, when the world is taking a turn for the worse, when turmoil is increasing, when trouble rises in my own life and family and fortunes, when everything appears to be against me and I am facing the consequences of a national spiritual drought, I will drink.

I will drink for my own health and for the health of those I love.

I will survive.

'He leads me beside the still waters.'

HE

Restores

MY

SOUL

There is a craze for restoration programmes in the UK. We love to see an old building rescued and restored and to watch the finest architects and interior designers give a whole new life to a beautiful home, whilst keeping its character.

We enjoy a little restoration ourselves, vicariously at least, through programmes which offer fashion tips, lifestyle coaching, makeovers, new hairstyles, diet and fitness regimes, and even cosmetic surgery. We may watch the more extreme TV series with a strange mixture of disapproval and fascination, but something intrigues us about a new lease of life, looking younger, finding an unexpected and more attractive side to ourselves: personal restoration and even transformation.

But there is one common theme in our culture which gives cause for disquiet. We are interested in everything that is physical. We are intent on improving our sex lives, refining our shape or our appearance. We love programmes about cookery, holidays, self-improvement, DIY, property and restoration.

But we neglect our souls. We are scarcely aware of our souls.

Like the notorious picture in the attic, in Oscar Wilde's *The Picture of Dorian Gray*, there is a true portrait of our souls hidden away, showing neglect, dissipation, the ravages of age and despair, whilst we go about town immaculately dressed, handsome and charming.

Yes, appearances do matter. But appearances, as we all know, can be deeply deceptive.

For too long, we have been obsessed by physical wellbeing to the neglect of our souls. Even if we don't subscribe to the idea of a 'soul', it is easy to see how billions of pounds are spent on medication, operations, all varieties of surgery, healthcare and hospital treatment. We spend an annual fortune on everything except… our nation's mental health.

Mental health services are truly the Cinderella of our society. We are obsessed with beautiful bodies but we have little or no concern for beautiful minds. Yet the statistics are overwhelming and frightening for the rapid rise in mental health problems among young people, an epidemic of depression, anorexia, bulimia, self-harm – and the still more shocking fact that the chief killer of men under the age of 45 in the UK is not cancer, not car accidents, but suicide (annually 6,000 and rising).

Our minds are in trouble not least because our souls are in trouble. We are steadily building the Tower of Babel in our world, the ultimate high-rise building of material aspiration. And it is on the shakiest foundation. Our dreams of money (the very fertile ground for the magical thinking of the National Lottery) and our obsession with celebrity, fame and beauty, are dangerous illusions. This is lethal when, in reality, our lives, our families and our finances are in such trouble.

The true portrait of Twenty-First Century Western society is decaying in the attic. We are becoming old and haggard beneath the make-up, and the contradiction between our inner and outer lives is set to destroy us.

'He restores my soul.'

Where is your soul? What is happening to it? Have you lost it? Where is it hiding?

The Hebrew word for 'soul' is *nefesh* and it means all of us – body, mind, personality, consciousness, everything that makes us who we are. It is not some disembodied ghost, lurking within our physical being. It is all connected; we are all one.

So to say a man is 'losing his soul' is really to say he is losing who he is. He is losing touch with his true identity. If the body takes on far too great an importance or if the mind, in the world of academic pride, starts to become monstrously large and the body is merely a device to carry this pulsating brain around, a man's soul is in disorder. If we lose harmony between all the aspects of our nature, then we are losing our soul. Our physical health matters, our mental health matters, and our personality and the growth of our character matters. Our values, our morality, our spiritual development matters.

It is one thing to engage in obsessive physical exercise during a lockdown, but it is another to pay attention to our souls. In recent times, inspirational videos and songs and the creativity of many artists have called us back to our true nature as spiritual beings.

If we lose sight of any area of our human identity, we are in danger of living half-lives. We are in danger of losing our soul.

'He restores my soul.'

I have long been engaged in a project to restore an ancient building in the far north of Scotland, and it is a delicate and painstaking process. But it is joyful and fulfilling too. I have discovered windows and even doors hidden in walls. I have discovered a Seventeenth Century fireplace hidden behind plaster, a hall concealed by Nineteenth Century partitions, beautiful old beams and ships' timbers lost beneath false ceilings.

Slowly, patiently, we are restoring the soul of this ancient and mysterious place.

But this is nothing compared to the blocked

windows that God wants to open in your life, the secret doors He wants you to discover, the forgotten hall where He wants you to blow away the dust and dance.

'He restores my soul.'

He wants to bring you back to who you are. He wants to reconnect you with every part of your being. He wants you to discover that you are made in the image of God.

He wants to wipe away the grime and the layers of terrible neglect from the shining glory of your original identity.

He wants you back.

'The Lord is my shepherd, I shall not want. He makes me to lie down in green pastures; he leads me beside the still waters, he restores my soul.'

HE LEADS

ME IN THE

PATHS OF

Righteousness,

FOR HIS

NAME'S SAKE

Righteousness is a very old-fashioned word and one that troubles us today. Sadly, we almost always hear it in a pejorative context now: 'She's so self-righteous.' 'I can't stand his appalling self-righteousness.'

But, occasionally, we catch a glimmer of what the word means. A reggae musician friend was touring the US with a Rastafarian friend and they were both staying at a hotel. As they stood on their balcony, they watched a very large teenage boy cross the courtyard with a huge bucket of Kentucky Fried Chicken, clearly all for himself. The Rastafarian singer turned to my friend and said, 'Man, that is so *unrighteous*!'

My sons and I laughed about this for a long time and it became a family phrase for many years. 'Man, that is so *unrighteous*!'

Who doesn't appreciate the dangers of excess? Of going too far, having too much, focusing on yourself to the exclusion of others?

Who hasn't fallen into such temptations? Haven't bankers, company directors and even chief executives of well-known charities waddled home with a massive Kentucky Fried Chicken bucket full of cash?

We have an instinct for what is out of proportion, what feels wrong, what feels right. We are not so ignorant, nor so apathetic that we don't have at least some sense of righteousness and unrighteousness in the world.

'He leads me in the paths of righteousness.'

Some translators put it like this: 'He leads me in the right paths.'

The problem with religious instruction is that it can become like those moments when you stop for directions (reluctantly if you're a man), and the person goes into great detail, with all the streets and landmarks clearly appearing before them as they speak – but not before you, unfortunately – so the 'turn second left at the top of the small hill, beside the old phone box' leads you into a wilderness of little avenues and cul-de-sacs, apparently with no way out…

But Psalm 23 does not talk about religious instruction or systems of faith or secondhand philosophies which might help. It says quite simply:

'He leads me in the paths of righteousness.'

He personally leads me
in the right way.

He gets in the car and says, 'Let me show you.'

How does this happen?

First of all, He refines our conscience. Too many of us have allowed this most sensitive of spiritual organs to become dull and unresponsive. The dark truth is, as any crime writer knows, the second murder is easier than the first, and the third straightforward, and the fourth a matter of course, and the fifth a habit.

Something that was once a struggle against our conscience, slowly, imperceptibly, becomes normal behaviour. Lying, unethical business practices, adultery: all these have small beginnings – a word, a thought, a look – but these 'micro-events' in the human heart, split-second thoughts and temptations, initially trouble a tender conscience. We feel instinctively, 'This is not right,' 'I should not do this, I should do that'. We are not moral psychopaths who have no history of feeling conscience-stricken, nor any empathy with our possible victims. But, once taken with difficulty, a 'wrong path' repeatedly taken can become a beaten track of sheer habit.

Slowly, we turn from creatures that are spiritually alive to those who live a half-life, wandering in the twilight of our own dreams and desires, full of self-justification. We have become experts at stifling our own consciences. Like inveterate smokers or alcoholics or drug addicts, we have reinforced our dangerous habits with illogical arguments and deep self-deception. But somehow it all works for us. It keeps us safely on the wrong path.

'He leads me in the paths of righteousness.'

He gives me back my conscience. 'Whether you

turn to the right or to the left, your ears will hear a voice behind you, saying, "This is the way; walk in it"' (Isaiah 30:21, NIV). There are many places in the Bible which sing of this truth and call us, lovingly and powerfully, to wake up from our dreams – to wake up from the nightmare of wrong paths which we know lead to self-destruction.

A tender conscience can certainly be a nuisance. It can become an irritation and may turn into our enemy if we are hell-bent on pursuing a wrong path. The first murder – the only murder most of us will ever commit – will be of our own conscience.

'He restores my soul.'

He gives us back a renewed conscience, when we take time, when we slow down, when we listen, when we rest, when we allow the Shepherd to lead us beside the still waters. Why does God have infinite patience with us? Why is it His very nature to be merciful, to forgive, to open new doors in our renovated hearts? Why does He long for us to start again, to turn back from the wrong paths we have taken and to be led, by Him, into paths of righteousness?

It is because He loves us far more than we can dare to imagine. No mother has ever loved, or indulged, or forgiven, or welcomed home, a wayward son or daughter with more tears and more happiness than God Himself. It is impossible to exaggerate His infinite love for us.

But there is one more reason why He leads us in the right paths…

For His name's sake.

This world is full of terrible adverts for God, horrible perversions of religion, of people who claim great authority but who kill and destroy, of powerful men and women who advocate vicious racism, suppression, punishment, violence, all in the name of their 'god'.

The world is full of religious frauds, and there is not one world religion or faith or tradition which is innocent of this charge.

The Creator of the universe, the great Shepherd of the sheep, is calling men, women and children to walk in right paths for His name's sake. He wants to proclaim His name and His authority, His love and power and holiness, in the midst of our troubled world.

He wants people who truly reflect His character, to walk in the ways of righteousness and let their whole lives sing with the music of eternity.

The words for righteousness and justice are interchangeable in Hebrew. There is no way we can be led into paths of righteousness without seeking justice and integrity in every area of our personal and national lives.

THE

Journey

SO FAR

We have reached the most important break in this song. The theme is about to turn darker, the music more sombre.

But we have been steadily prepared and strengthened for the extreme weather ahead. The Creator of the universe Himself is our guide.

The Lord is my shepherd.

He is my shepherd and I will always hold onto this truth in life and in death. He is mine and I am His.

I shall not want.

He provides me with everything I need for life's journey.

He makes me to lie down in green pastures.

His love provides an environment of perfect safety, no matter what has happened in my life before.

He leads me beside the still waters.

He will open up a long-forgotten well of fresh water even in the worst desert of my experience. He will lead me to drink and I will never be thirsty again.

He restores my soul.

He will uncover the glorious image of divine beauty beneath all the grime and the years of neglect. He will renovate my heart and give me new hope for the future.

He leads me in the paths of righteousness for His name's sake.

He will lead me in the right paths, He will forgive me for all of the wrong paths I have taken. He will never let me go finally astray because of His eternal love for me and because He has chosen me to be an ambassador for His true character. This is my destiny, to become like Him.

There is nothing that life or death can throw at me that can drown out the most beautiful song in the world:

'The Lord is my shepherd.'

YEA, THOUGH

I WALK

Through

the valley

OF THE

SHADOW OF

DEATH

This is one of the most famous phrases in the whole of world literature. It is full of foreboding and horror. It is not surprising that a comedian once said, 'Yea though I walk... No, I will run through the valley of the shadow of death.'

But we can't run. And sometimes it seems that we have pitched camp there, and we live for many years in this terrible, sunless place. There is no escaping the harsh realities of our lives.

The trouble with some kinds of religion is that they offer a panacea, a kind of drug of endless praising and celebration and joy, a draught of holy oblivion which can seem to obliterate our sorrows. But this kind of relief is very temporary and such hyped-up enthusiasm can be alienating and dangerously destructive. An irreligious person may be tempted to drown their sorrows with drink or empty hedonism, but a religious person can equally try to drown their sorrows in a whirlwind of religious activity or even a severe and stoical application to religious duty: 'I must carry on whatever.'

But underneath everything we try, every distraction, every technique, every activity whether spiritual or material... underneath is the valley, where we are still walking.

I grew up near Liverpool and I still support Liverpool Football Club. When I hear the resounding anthem on TV, 'You'll never walk alone' it makes me nostalgic for those days on the terraces at the Kop. This is a beautiful song in its own right, even when sung with the harsh voices of thousands of football fans. It was incredibly moving when this song was sung by Michael Ball and the 100-year-old Captain Tom Moore to support NHS workers in the midst of the national pandemic. But, in spite of these great inspirational moments, when we are truly in the valley of the shadow of death there is no doubt that part of the sheer anguish is that we experience this journey alone. We feel, at the deepest level, that we are alone and no one can rescue us from the grief or the loss we are experiencing. Our generation will understand this better than any which have gone before, because of the devastating solitude of people dying from COVID-19.

It is a truism that we are 'born alone and we die alone'. Family, friendship, love, marriage, business partnerships, team sports, even the camaraderie of soldiers at war, all give us a sense of belonging, a strength in numbers, a feeling of hope against the odds. But when we walk through the valley of the shadow of death, we can feel that the odds are against us and that we are truly alone.

There is no one to walk with us, because they cannot truly understand what is happening to us. This goes for the loss of a child, the tragic death of a husband or wife, the suicide of a loved one, the horror of a girlfriend being raped and killed, the murder of a whole family by terrorists and the extremes of war. But it also goes for the living death of divorce, the devastations of adultery and betrayal, the collapse of a business partnership through fraud or greed, the abandonment by friends, family feuds and rejection by children, financial collapse, the loss of dreams and the end of hope.

'Yea, though I walk through the valley of the shadow of death…'

One of the first books I ever remember was a massive ancient Victorian volume of *The Pilgrim's Progress* by John Bunyan. I was too young to read when I opened this book – I must have been about three – but I will never forget staring at the old engraving of 'The Valley of the Shadow of Death'. It was full of dreadful monsters, horrible mutant creatures like something out of Hieronymus Bosch. There were demonic figures in the darkness, lurking in the shadows, beneath rocks, emerging from clefts in the ground. It was truly a dismal and surreal landscape for a three-year-old's imagination, and the fact that I am writing about it

65 years later shows the sheer level of impact on my innocent mind.

How could there be such horrors? Who could protect me? What was this evil place? Was this a nightmare or a real place in the world?

But as I stared at this scenario with fatal fascination, did I imagine any of the real life tragedies and horrors that lay ahead for me? My world was safe, with loving parents. I had no doubt that my father could kill those monsters if they attacked our home.

But when it came to it, my parents could not prevent the collapse and death of my marriage, they could not save my third child lost in late pregnancy, they could not intervene to save a cousin killed by a drunken driver in the most horrific circumstances. They could do nothing to avert the pain and humiliation of financial collapse, business betrayals and ruined projects, all of which have blighted my life at different times.

And finally, what could my mother do for anyone, after a lifetime of helping others, when she descended into that darkest valley of Alzheimer's disease and no longer remembered my name?

'You'll never walk alone…'

That's not how we feel when we walk in the valley of the shadow of death. It is the very place where all possibility of love, belief and the very existence of

God are tested in a dreadful fire, a cold and pitiless fire, a freezing world of burning desolation. It is the place where atheists quarry their most cogent arguments against any God of love.

The suffering we go through, the suffering throughout the whole world, is a knock-down argument against any light or hope or love or benevolence at the heart of the universe.

'Yea, though I walk through the valley of the shadow of death.'

This greatest of all songs does not plunge us into the darkness without preparing us first. We travel on the road of self-discovery, of restoration and hope first. Only then are we ready to put into context the very worst and most challenging aspects of our lives on earth. Nor does the song leave us there, in the minor key, in the world of the tragic symphony or the terrible clashing of a dissonant and despairing contemporary anguish. We will eventually pass through the valley into what Churchill once called, in the darkest days of the war, 'sunlit uplands'.

It is easy to forget that my parents – who could not save me from the troubles of my own life – knew even more about darkness and despair than I did. They both fought in a terrible war against Hitler when it seemed that hope and light would die for ever. When Churchill talked of 'sunlit uplands' they knew it was a far-off dream.

But they believed the dream and they fought for it. My mother was in the crowd on VE Day in London when Churchill waved his famous victory 'V' from the balcony at Buckingham Palace and the whole of Britain was in a frenzy of celebration. But many millions did not live to see that day, including people who continued to recite this psalm in the pitch night of the Nazi death camps.

When I worked on an animated film for Channel 4 about the Jewish faith, the young Jewish director chose to dramatise her own father and grandfather's experience in Auschwitz. Faced with the celebration of Passover and no food, in the midst of all that terror, the grandfather drew a Seder plate in chalk on an empty table. He drew a Passover cup. He drew the unleavened bread, the *matzo*, and the lamb and the bitter herbs. They ate an imaginary Passover meal in the valley of the shadow of death.

My mother was in the ATS (Auxiliary Territorial Service) and entered the devastated city of Cologne with Number One Brigade in 1945. She was shocked at the truly terrible aftermath of the war and the horrific discoveries of those dark days. Somewhere, in the smoking ruins of that city, another small discovery was made – a simple inscription.

A Jewish citizen had scratched these words on

the wall of a cellar, whilst hiding from the terror of deportation to the Nazi death camps:

> **'I believe in the sun even**
> **when it is not shining.**
> **I believe in love even**
> **when I cannot feel it.**
> **I believe in God even**
> **when he is silent.'**

Is such remarkable courage just a form of madness and self-delusion?

As we walk through the valley of the shadow of death, with our own sorrows, terrors and desperations, we must face many questions.

Elie Wiesel, who wrote the book *Night* about his own experience of the death camps, said that the question was not 'Where was God?' but 'Where was man?'

Before we question the whereabouts of God, we may want to question the whereabouts of some of the most influential leaders and thinkers of our day. They may be more lost than we are.

I WILL

FEAR

No evil,

FOR YOU

ARE WITH

ME

This is one of the most dramatic changes in any of the great songs, which we call the Psalms. In the first six verses, the singer speaks of the Shepherd in the third person: 'He makes me to lie down in green pastures, he leads me… He restores my soul.'

But now, it's personal. It's sudden and intimate. It's 'you' not 'he'.

In the midst of the darkness, he turns to the Shepherd and says, 'you'.

The Authorised Version of the Bible keeps the ancient distinction, well-known in French (*tu* and *vous*) and German (*du* and *sie*), between the intimate address 'thou' and the more respectful and polite 'you'.

The singer is on direct and intimate terms with his Lord. 'I will fear no evil, for thou art with me.'

I will fear no evil, because you are close, you are beside me, you know me better than anyone on earth and you love me completely.

One of my greatest and most influential friends, the Rev. David Watson, wrote a book called *Fear No Evil* when he was dying of cancer. I am one of many who still miss him after more than 30 years, but one of his many legacies was the gift of these words, which came from the valley of the shadow of death. David hoped and believed he was going to be healed, but when the healing proved to be elusive and, finally, a false hope, he placed his true hope in the Good Shepherd with these words:

'I will fear no evil for you are with me.'

It is common to think that love and hate are opposites, but it would be more accurate to say that love and fear are opposites. Fear tends to drive out love.

For many of us the feeling of insecurity which dominates our lives goes right back to a deep and devastating sense that we are not safe, we are not held – someone is going to drop us, or hurt us, or change their mood and suddenly turn on us. We have no rock, no safe haven, no mother or father who truly holds us in every situation of threat, in every storm or shock that life can bring. We feel that they will simply let us go and, in many cases, they do. We are alone in our bedroom, afraid, and no one comes. We are stumbling through life as a teenager but our father is much too busy to notice. He doesn't see the signs of our distress. He doesn't notice the anorexia until it's too late, or the depression, until it's too far gone, or the self-harm until it becomes blindingly obvious.

He doesn't realise that we are on our iPhones in

the middle of the night, overwhelmed with forces of social media and cyber-bullying.

We are not held. Our parents are not there.

'I will fear no evil, for you are with me.'

You… The Shepherd… God Himself, the Creator of the universe, He is there. He is close. He is never not there.

This is the greatest truth any young person can ever discover.

My parents were not there, for huge portions of my life, because I was at boarding school, where I was deeply unhappy and, at times, terrifyingly alone.

But it was in this context that I discovered the truth of Psalm 23. I began to experience a presence with me, even though I was physically alone. A loving presence that truly cared.

This happened because I started to read the Bible.

'I will fear no evil, for you are with me.'

One of the problems of a certain kind of British or American culture is a tendency towards over-optimism. In Britain, it often manifests itself through a 'stiff upper lip': 'Keep going and things will turn out OK.' 'Nothing is that bad.' 'Don't make a fuss.' 'Keep on keeping on!' There is a certain stoical reserve, a tendency to brush problems under the carpet and minimise a problem. 'It's not that bad.'

This is a serious mistake and it is obvious, in the world of medicine, that an over-optimistic diagnosis can prove fatal. 'It's not that bad.' 'It's just indigestion; it's just acid reflux,' as a friend of mine was told by a GP weeks before he was rushed into hospital suffering from pancreatic cancer. My own son was told three times by a GP, over a period of 18 months, 'Your stomach pains are not appendicitis, but probably some kind of stomach virus'. When he was finally rushed into hospital, his appendix had gone gangrenous and he narrowly escaped peritonitis and possibly death.

Wrong diagnosis. 'It's not that bad.'

It may be that British and American deaths from COVID-19 have been so high because of an over-optimistic approach to the initial crisis. But it is not just our political leaders who have been guilty of too much optimism; many of us have the same kind of tendency to exaggerate the positive. I heard it said by a confident speaker, a few years ago, that 'so much good is happening in the world that no one born in 2015 would prefer to have been born 20 years earlier'.

A boy in Syria? A Yazidi family in Iraq? A little girl whose grandparents have been killed in a bush fire in Western Australia?

The idea that the world is always getting progressively better is just as dangerous as the idea that the world is always getting worse.

The fact is, human nature remains unchanged and has potential for both good and evil.

Evil.

Yes, it exists.

'I will fear no evil because it doesn't exist.' Somehow that doesn't ring true. 'I will fear no evil because the world is always getting better.' No.

'I will fear no evil because you are with me.'

The power of evil is a mystery. Is there such a reality beyond the worst human actions? Are there dark powers at work, at a cosmic level?

Many religions believe in such forces. A great many people no longer believe in them.

But, whatever you believe, the word 'evil' has not gone away in the Twenty-First Century and the concept of deep darkness erupting through psychopathic dictators, or human greed leading to the devastation of the planet, or the rise of human trafficking, or even the mundane cruelty of adultery, or domestic abuse, or the horrible prevalence of racism, child sexual abuse…

Evil is out there. It is real.

But there is always hope, which is something very different from over-optimism. There is always a way forward, but not by minimising evil or denying its existence or playing it down, or pretending that 'it's not so bad' or fooling ourselves that the world is always and inevitably getting better.

There is always hope, but only when we diagnose a problem correctly.

There is such a place as the valley of the shadow of death. At some time in my life, now or in the future, I will have to walk through it. But I will not be afraid.

'I will fear no evil, for you are with me.'

YOUR

ROD AND

YOUR STAFF,

THEY

Comfort

me

There is no doubt that this was the most difficult line in the whole psalm for me, until I understood its true meaning.

How could a 'rod' be comforting?

I grew up in the 1950s and 1960s when corporal punishment was still commonplace. I was beaten several times at school. There was an ancient proverb which was often quoted ominously by teachers or parents, 'Spare the rod and spoil the child.'

This is a controversial subject even in the Twenty-First Century, because for thousands of years children have been beaten as a form of discipline – and not just beaten but punished in a wide variety of ways. Some people still think this is acceptable and put down the problems of bad behaviour in the modern world to the lack of retribution: 'Bring back the cane!' It is not surprising that the very idea of authority has become associated with punishment – parents and teachers may offer the occasional reward, perhaps, but they always hold the power and the threat of punishment. They hold the rod.

Some people cannot think of their own fathers without a feeling of darkness, a cloud of judgment and, in many cases, they have experienced far more random acts of violence than formal discipline. Many people have been physically abused. Tragically, in recent decades, the terrible truth has emerged that figures in authority, parents, relatives, teachers, priests, have sexually abused huge numbers of young people; physical, sexual, emotional abuse has been prolific.

A dark cloud hangs over the church, throughout the world. No wonder many people reject God.

'Your rod and Your staff, they comfort me.' How can this be true?

Is the discipline of the Shepherd somehow a bizarre kind of comfort, a reassurance that He cares for us?

No. This is completely wrong.

When did you ever see a shepherd using a rod to beat the sheep?

The rod is not a stick to beat the sheep. It is a weapon in the hands of the shepherd to defend the sheep against wild animals, predators, thieves and rustlers who come to steal and destroy.

The Shepherd is our champion. He is our defender. He is on our side. He is not sitting in judgment over us and He is not meting out punishments, beating us and abusing us and condemning us.

He is not like any earthly figure of authority who

wields a stick and delivers threats and sentences people to beatings or prison or execution.

He is a warrior-shepherd, who will stop at nothing to save the sheep.

'The Lord is my shepherd, I shall not want.'

I shall not lack anything, including protection.

The Shepherd has a rod to defend us and a staff to guide us, gently, into the right paths. We are familiar with the symbol of the shepherd's crook, the curved staff which is used to pull the wandering sheep back into the fold, back into safety.

It is a dreadful irony when a bishop is accused of bullying or physical or sexual abuse, because the bishop carries the shepherd's staff as his or her most powerful sign: they are there to guide the sheep and to keep them safe. From a moral and spiritual point of view, those in high authority also need the rod as well as the staff; they need to be warriors of justice, defending the vulnerable and the innocent. They need to speak out, to declare the truth, to expose evil, to courageously defend their flock.

The Lord is my shepherd and He knows how to wield the rod with the lightning speed of a martial arts champion.

God is on your side. He is for you, not against you. He is your champion. He is your defender, even when every figure of authority lets you down, fails you, disappoints you, threatens you and abuses you.

The more you sing this song, the more this psalm goes deeper and deeper into your soul, the more you will know and live this truth.

We all carry wounds, sometimes from so deep in our childhood that we only know the effects of the terrible hurt – we cannot even remember the cause. But the Shepherd knows and He will defend us in the world of memory. He will be our champion in the past and the present and the future.

I had an experience of this myself. When I was about eight or nine, I told my parents that I had a memory of being locked into a cupboard and it was dark and there was no light switch. I was trying to explain the extreme fear of the dark which I had – a fear which continued throughout my teenage years and beyond. My parents, who were good and loving people, assured me that nothing like this could ever have happened to me.

They would never have shut me in a cupboard. They would never have punished me in such a heartless way. Gradually, they convinced me that my memory was false. Perhaps it was a dream, some nightmare from long ago. The years went by and the fear of the dark continued. I even sought help from psychiatrists and psychotherapists when I was a student.

I was afraid of punishment and judgment. Like so

many of us, I had grown up with a confusion in my mind. Authority was mixed up with judgment and around my parents, around teachers and around the very idea of God Himself was the threat of punishment. The threat of the dark.

I believe that many people who declare that they do not believe in God are rejecting a harsh figure of judgment and punishment. And when people tell me of such things, I have often said, 'I agree with you. I do not believe in this god either.'

'He makes me to lie down in green pastures; He leads me beside the still waters. He restores my soul.'

I believe in the God who is love, who defends me against all evil, who guides me into the paths of righteousness.

'Your rod and Your staff, they comfort me.'

The story about my childhood nightmare, being locked in the cupboard, is not finished. I carried this vague and troubling memory with me for many years and, if I ever mentioned it occasionally to my parents, it was always the same reply: 'We would never have let that happen to you.' But when I was 40, I went with my parents to visit a very old lady who had looked after me when I was a small child. Dorothy Dawson was fiercely loyal to me and always called me 'my Murray'. I called her Darty, because aged two I hadn't been able to say her name properly and it stuck. 'Darty.' She was 90 when we visited her and full of stories. We laughed and enjoyed the nostalgic reminiscences of long ago. But then, out tumbled one story which had a huge impact on my life and shocked my parents. I won't use the woman's real name, but... 'That Jane Wilson,' said Darty, 'that woman who looked after you while I was having a baby, she was a dreadful woman! She couldn't cope with you! If you cried or made a fuss, she would lock you in the cupboard and you would scream to come out but she would leave you in there for hours!' You can imagine the silence in the room when Darty finished her story, which included finding me at the age of two and a half wandering alone in the street, filthy and bedraggled, and taking me home.

My parents 'would never have done anything like that'. But they had been very busy when I was little, and I had been left in the care of two people, one good and one bad.

I mention this personal story, because I still consider it rather a miracle that I ever found out the truth. I did not have a false memory. I had not made up a story. And there was a disturbing logic to the terror of the dark that haunted me for so many decades.

I believe that this discovery was one case when the Lord who is my shepherd took His rod and entered the world of my distant past and swung His cudgel to defeat the demon of fear.

We are all victims of human sinfulness, including our own. We are vulnerable to our parents' mistakes, if not their abuses. We all have stories to tell. And we all need a defender.

And, finally, we all desperately need comfort. That is something which was sadly lacking in the many long years I spent away at boarding school. But that was also where I discovered the truth that 'The Lord is my shepherd'.

'Your rod and Your staff, they comfort me.'

God is not a punitive God. He is not about threat and punishment. I believe that the Hebrew Scriptures need to be read through the lens of this psalm and many other passages of tender love, forgiveness and protection. Here is the truth at the heart of the universe.

YOU

Prepare a
table before

ME IN THE

PRESENCE OF

MY ENEMIES

This is one of the most puzzling and beautiful lines in our 3000 year-old lyric.

Some people might see this as a vindictive picture: we are given a banquet, eating and drinking our fill, to taunt our enemies. They look on hungrily and despondently from a distance. We can get our revenge; we can torment them with our success.

This is a childish misinterpretation. We need to go back to the very beginning of the psalm: 'The Lord is my shepherd.'

Sometimes, this psalm is treated as two halves: the first is about the shepherd and the sheep, and the second is about God and the human soul. But the imagery of the shepherd must be carried right through every verse.

Middle Eastern shepherds still have names for different valleys, cliffs and landmarks. One route might easily be called 'The Valley of the Shadow of Death' because it is so dark and dangerous, another 'Skull Cliff', another 'the Jackal's Lair' and another 'Pathway of the Lilies' or 'Green Pastures.' It is easy to see how David, the shepherd boy, found his imagery.

The Shepherd leads me through the shadow of death, protecting me all the way. Now He takes me to a level and fertile place, but there are still caves and cliffs and boulders and places where predators can lie in wait. He takes me to where there is succulent grass and a fresh spring of water, a place to revive my spirits, 'The Table in the Wilderness'.

'You prepare a table before me.'

It is not just at the beginning of the psalm that the Shepherd finds green pastures and still waters; it is right in the midst of the threats and the troubles and the fears. He never stops finding oases for us, places of rest, moments of pure peace.

The Shepherd is life-giving and even when we feel overwhelmed by despair or thoughts of death, even in the midst of bereavement and tragedy, or facing overwhelming troubles, He will still prepare a table for us. He will show us that we can feed safely under His protection, in the presence of our enemies.

Who are these enemies?

For sheep in the ancient Middle East they are numerous: wolves, lions, jackals, snakes.

But picture the Shepherd, guarding us as we eat and drink peacefully, perhaps lighting a fire to ward off the savage creatures, creating a haven of tranquillity – right in the midst of the terrible threat.

We learn that the presence of the Shepherd is far more powerful than 'the presence of my enemies'.

What is happening here is a heightened experience of green pastures, a truth we can take through every day of our lives, no matter what is happening, or how deep the suffering or how great the threats.

'You prepare a table for me in the presence of my enemies.'

Many of the great psalms talk about 'enemies', and for King David and many of the psalm-singers these enemies were literal opponents, armed assassins who were seeking to kill and destroy. But it is important to read the Psalms with the deepest insight and to recognise, as all the great religions do, that enemies are often within. They are not out there, but they arise from our own subconscious, from our wounded spirits, from our fearful imaginations.

We face the enemies of fear, of crippling anxiety, of low self-esteem, of oppression, of addiction, of bitterness, of resentment... and to these deadly foes, we must add all the vices that threaten our spiritual health: pride, greed, lust, self-righteousness, gluttony, envy, self-obsession.

We have a great many enemies and most of them are inside, deep down, flourishing in the darkness of our own heart.

Recent decades have seen a dreadful pattern of hostility between opposing countries, ideologies and political positions. Nations like the USA and Britain have become bitterly divided and accusations are constantly flying between different groups, with hatred and venom pouring out in 'Twitter-storms.'

It is always more comfortable to see the enemy 'out there' – it's someone else, it's another race, another religion, another party, another country.

When we are invited to eat a banquet in the presence of our enemies, we are called to the most powerful kind of spiritual nourishment which can protect us from enemies, inside and out, a banquet which has the fruits of love and forgiveness and hope and peace.

It is a table spread in very difficult and dangerous terrain. We are called to feed our minds and our consciences and our souls with divine inspiration that can change the way we think and act. It is a banquet which will destroy evil.

'You prepare a table for me in the presence of my enemies.'

YOU

ANOINT

My head

WITH

OIL

For thousands of years, Middle Eastern shepherds have gathered their flocks into the fold at night, carefully examining every sheep for scratches, cuts or sores. They have cleaned the wounds and poured oil to soothe and heal.

This psalm takes us on a journey from green pastures to dark shadows, from still waters, to raging despair. As we travel through the valley of the shadow of death, we may well be wounded; our souls and our minds may suffer great anguish. We are fed and watered, protected by the Shepherd, 'in the presence of our enemies', but deep down we are crying out for healing.

Now it comes. Now the Lord bends down to us and carefully looks at every single wound and cleans it and drops the most soothing oil into the most painful and hidden places.

How can such healing happen?

It starts by not hiding any more. It starts by not pretending any more. It starts when we stop behaving like proud individuals who must cope on their own and must never reveal weakness. It starts when we recognise that we are sheep and we have a shepherd.

Our Shepherd is the great healer of the human race.

The whole world is crying out for healing, but many are forsaking the Shepherd or ignoring His loving call, the sweet music of the most beautiful song in the world:

'The Lord is my shepherd.'

We have no other guardian and we have no other healer.

In the Twenty-First Century, we have the most advanced physical remedies, we have life-saving surgery, we have a thousand medications and the most sophisticated technology and billions of dollars are poured every year into cancer research. With astonishing speed, we developed vaccines for COVID-19. And we may develop vaccines for the next pandemic and the next.

One day, we may beat physical disease.

But who will heal the troubled soul? Who will save the human race from its mental affliction?

I have no doubt that every verse of this psalm is oil to be poured onto our deepest wounds. It is one of the greatest and deepest reassurances that God is with us.

We must allow the Shepherd to inspect our wounds, our sorrows, our hidden guilt, our secret sins, our mental anguish, our vague unease, our deepening depression, our confusion, our disappointed longings, our agonised cries for love and forgiveness.

We must start here, in this place, with these simple words.

The Lord is my shepherd, I shall not want. I shall not lack for anything. He will provide all that I need, including healing. He will pour oil onto my raging wounds.

He will give me the courage to share my troubles with someone else. He will speak to me through others, who have travelled this way before. He will open new pathways for me – 'He will guide me in the paths of righteousness.' He will lead me into the fold and look lovingly and with great care at the wounds I cannot even see myself. He will anoint me with oil.

Community is very important when it comes to healing. Anyone who has followed a 12-step programme knows this. It starts with admitting the problem: 'My name is John and I am an alcoholic.' It acknowledges that I cannot heal myself. It encourages me to trust in a Higher Power and it gives me a fellowship of suffering and sympathetic friendship, regular meetings with others who are on the spiritual journey.

The Lord is my shepherd and He will lead me to people and organisations and religious communities that care, if I will only follow Him. If I will only give up trying to cope by myself. If I will only stop pretending and stop hiding my wounds.

When He pours the oil, it will set me free to be honest and to cooperate with my healing, and to seek help or eventually give help to others.

Psalm 23 is very much an individual journey: 'I will fear no evil for you are with me.' It is about me. It is about the Shepherd and me. But all this is to place me, as a restored person, as a healed person, into a community of love.

That is why the second and most familiar meaning of this verse is consecration.

Queen Elizabeth II took her own anointing, at the coronation in 1953, so seriously that no television cameras were allowed to witness it. She considered this ancient rite of consecration so sacred that it must be private, a matter between her and God.

For thousands of years, from the time of Aaron in the Hebrew Scriptures, priests and kings have been anointed with oil.

'He anoints my head with oil.'

The Shepherd consecrates us to His service, He raises us up high and says, 'You are chosen. I love you. I have always loved you, before the beginning of time. You have a purpose on this earth and I am anointing you to fulfil your destiny.'

Our destiny will always be far more than the pursuit of our own happiness. It will be to live a life of love and sacrifice for others. We are called to be ambassadors of love and healing power wherever we are and, in fulfilling this destiny, we will be happy.

'He anoints my head with oil.'

He heals me and He consecrates me. He cares for me and He chooses me to be His companion, His friend and His ambassador.

MY CUP

Overflows

Hospitality is one of the greatest art forms.

To welcome others into our homes, however humble, is to offer a gift which can be healing and life-changing.

In the ancient Middle East, it was customary to anoint the head of the visitor with oil, to wash his dusty feet and then to give him food and wine.

The wine would be poured into a goblet until it overflowed, as a wonderful sign that the hospitality would be truly generous – that nothing would be lacking.

'The Lord is my shepherd, I shall not want.' 'My cup overflows.'

This is one of the most beautiful images of the psalm... a cup of wine, overflowing, welling up, never failing.

It is common for people to see religion as taking things away, banning happiness, laughter, dancing, joy.

And, sadly, that has often been the case. My mother was brought up in the Plymouth Brethren and she was not allowed to go to the cinema or wear make-up or drink alcohol or go to parties or attend the theatre or, most dangerous of all, she was utterly forbidden to visit a dance hall!

Dancing, somehow, seemed the greatest vice, perhaps because it was too sensual, too physical, bringing men and women together in scenes of wild abandon. A friend, who attended a Dutch Reformed university in the USA, which had very strict behaviour codes for the students, told me that this saying went around: 'You should not have sex before marriage, because it might lead to dancing.'

I laughed a lot at this satirical comment. But there is a tragedy underlying all this – a life half-lived, the danger of defining the spiritual journey in negative terms: 'This is what I don't do; this is what I don't say.'

But what *do* you do? And where is the joy? Where is the overflowing cup?

My mother bravely overcame many of the restrictions of her childhood. (It's almost comical to think that the cinema she was not allowed to visit was the world of Charlie Chaplin, Laurel and Hardy and Rudolph Valentino.) She did start going to the theatre and she even took a degree in English Literature at the University of London. One strict Baptist friend was very concerned for her and gave her this warning: 'All poetry is of the devil.' This is rather embarrassing for the Bible, a huge proportion of which is poetry – including Psalm 23.

My mother rose far beyond ridiculous prejudices. But there was one that still lingered. Although we were taken, as children, to see great plays at the Liverpool Playhouse and great concerts at the Royal Liverpool Philharmonic, we never saw any ballet or dance.

I was fortunate to have a school friend who became a ballet dancer, eventually dancing with Ballet Rambert, so I had a late education in the glories of dance. I have directed quite a number of musicals and worked with brilliant choreographers and dancers, so I have reclaimed some of this lost territory in the family history. But I still can't dance, and nothing fills me with more dread than being pulled up onto the dance floor at a wedding or a party!

In her final years, my mother had Alzheimer's disease, but there was a very touching moment when one of her carers asked her, 'Dorothy, do you have any regrets?' My 97-year-old mother thought hard and, out of the fog of her dementia, came this reply: 'I wish I had danced.'

I wish I had danced.

'My cup overflows'.

Here, in Psalm 23, is the most fabulous invitation to live life to the full. Here is a celebration of hospitality, of artistry, of music, of humour.

I believe everything is contained in these words.

Any religious life, or spiritual journey, which is largely about negatives, 'thou shalt nots', rules, regulations, self-denial, without any sense of joy or celebration, has missed the point entirely.

Any family or human community which lacks laughter, which is far too serious and intense and self-obsessed, is not only a harmful environment but is potentially dangerous. The worst ideologies and crimes against humanity have come from legalistic, controlling, humourless and dark kingdoms of self-obsession and rampant egotism.

Laughter liberates. And like the wine, in this precious verse, it overflows – the best laughter is uncontrollable.

Love is uncontrollable. It pours over the brim, it keeps on pouring. There is no limit to its generosity and it extends to the unlovable, to the awkward, to the marginalised, even to our enemies. Love cannot be stopped or limited.

'My cup overflows'.

This is an image of the Spirit of God pouring into the human soul and filling our whole lives with incredible richness and kindness and fun and praise... and dancing.

King David became so euphoric during a

procession into Jerusalem that the Hebrew Scriptures record that 'David danced naked before the ark' (2 Sam 6.14). Such a scene would have been my maternal grandparents' very worst nightmare and it would have justified all their deepest suspicions. The human body, out of control, in public! Even at the time, David's wife Michal was so shocked and offended that she poured scorn on him.

But it remains an incredible image of abandonment, in the presence of God.

Remember that David wrote this psalm.

He wrote the most beautiful song in the world.

'My cup overflows'.

He knew what he was talking about.

SURELY

GOODNESS

AND MERCY

Shall

follow me

ALL THE DAYS

OF MY LIFE

When I was 10 years old, my parents bought a house in North Wales. It was a very beautiful cottage with views over the Clwyd Vale and it was right beside a sheep farm. I loved to watch the farmer whistling and shouting commands to his sheep dogs – 'Come by, come by!' – as they rounded up the sheep. I was fascinated by the incredible alertness of the border collies, their speed, their instant obedience to their master.

In the coming years, there was a BBC programme called *One Man and His Dog*, where shepherds from all over the country would demonstrate the brilliance and the astonishing skills of their dogs – it seemed like the ultimate expression of a 'man's best friend'. This exclusively male world of shepherds and dogs (the dogs were often female of course) was summed up bluntly in the title, *One Man and His Dog*. That was until a lovely childhood friend of mine, Katy Cropper, became a shepherdess in the Lake District, entered the programme and famously won the competition! We were incredibly proud of her, and her mother told me, a few years ago, that Katy had been asked by the Mayor of London to bring a flock of sheep and herd them, with her sheepdogs, over London Bridge. This was to celebrate the ancient anniversary of the 'Freedom of London', a very high honour, which includes the right to herd your own sheep into the city!

Not content with 40 years of watching the sheep farmers in North Wales and many years of following Katy's illustrious career, I bought a sheepdog in 2004 and she lived in the far north of Scotland with me and my family for more than 15 years. I can honestly say that she taught me more about faithfulness, loyalty and love than almost anyone, in my whole life. I mourn the loss of her every day.

I sometimes think there should be paintings of 'The Birds Preaching to St Francis' or 'Dogs Demonstrating Divine Truths to Wayward Humans'...

The animal kingdom has so much to tell us.

But there was one rare moment when a preacher in our little Baptist chapel in North Wales allowed the dogs to have their divine moment. It was 50 years ago but I can still remember his sermon on Psalm 23, for when he came to this verse: 'Surely goodness and mercy shall follow me all the days of my life,' he pictured those two wonderful virtues as Welsh Border Collies.

'Goodness' and 'Mercy' will follow us, like sheepdogs, directing us, guiding us, herding us to safety, obeying the commands of the Lord, following us forever.

Sheepdogs have incredible loyalty and, typically, they are loyal to one person. They are loyal to their master or mistress. They have the most wonderful faithfulness and here, in this verse, the deepest concept of faithfulness is embedded in the Hebrew word *hesed* – which is translated as 'mercy'. *Hesed* is sometimes translated as 'loving-kindness' in the older versions of the Bible, or 'love and faithfulness'. Like *shalom*, which means so much more than 'peace', *hesed* is hard to translate.

But 'mercy' is beautiful in this context.

Goodness is what we need: a powerful, protective goodness, the outpouring of God's character and goodwill and holiness all around us. And mercy is what we long for most: to be accepted, to be forgiven, to be held in absolute unconditional love.

Pope Francis, some years ago, proclaimed the 'Year of Mercy', and he believes that mercy is the crown of all divine qualities. It sums up everything.

To receive mercy, constantly, daily, to be on the receiving end of God's 'loving kindness', and to give mercy to others, to give mercy generously, to forgive, to be merciful, is to be truly blessed.

It is impossible to exaggerate the spiritual power of mercy.

The world is in desperate need of goodness and mercy, and so are we. All radical change, all spiritual revolutions, must begin in the human heart. They must begin with us, alone on our spiritual journey.

They must begin with a life that walks through the valley of the shadow of death, that rejoices in a banquet of God's love even when enemies and fears and threats surround us; revolutions must start when one person receives a cup that is brimming over with the glory and the generosity of God and when one person walks bravely through the world, followed by goodness and mercy…

For one life, surrounded by goodness and mercy, driven onwards, guided through the uncertain future, is infectious in the best possible way. Such a life is filled with the contagion of divine love which must spread rapidly from one heart to another, one family to another.

We live in a world which is not only threatened by pandemics but also by raging forest fires.

More than ever, we need goodness and mercy to follow us and to spread the fire of their influence and to inform our actions and to create whole cultures of hope and goodness and justice and care for the planet and care for one another. We need a raging fire of love in the world.

But it starts with a fire burning in the human heart.

My paternal grandfather's memorial window has a burning human heart at its centre and ever since that was installed in his church in 1959, I have been fascinated with that picture.

In recent years, I came across St Teresa of Avila's concept of 'the exchange of hearts'. It goes something like this. 'God says to us, "Give me your heart", with all your longings, your fears, your worries, your wounds, your needs and your hopes. I will look after your heart, I will heal you, I will provide for you. But trust me… Trust me with your heart.

'And in exchange, I will give you my heart. I will give you my heart for the world, my love for others, my overflowing love for children, for the poor, for outsiders, for the unlovely and my faithful love even for the harsh and violent and lost souls of this world. I will give you my heart, which is open to everyone. Which is always flowing and always brimming with goodness, mercy and pure love.'

Surely goodness and mercy will follow me all the days of my life. What a vision! What hope for you and me!

What hope for the world.

It was the former Chief Rabbi Jonathan Sacks, who said, 'We need to create ecologies of hope.' We need to create environments in which hope is likely to flourish.

This planting, this tending and nurturing of hope must surely begin at home.

And there is no better place to start than by singing the most beautiful song in the world.

'Surely goodness and mercy will follow me all the days of my life'.

AND I

WILL DWELL

IN THE

HOUSE OF

THE LORD

Forever.

A Russian artist, Alexej von Jawlensky, wrote at the beginning of the Twentieth Century, 'All art is nostalgia for God.'

It is a haunting phrase, particularly for an age that was about to lose itself in the horrors of war and to spend most of the century trying to find its way spiritually and emotionally – a quest that has continued, even at the height of technological brilliance and material prosperity.

The word 'nostalgia' really means 'the pain of longing to go home'.

Perhaps one of the most famous sayings, after the time of the Bible, was written in AD 386 by a very brilliant and confused young man who was trying to find his way back to God. He wrote, 'Our hearts are restless until they find their rest in Thee.' He was the first great writer to use the word 'confessions' as the title for a book.

I grew up in the 1960s and 1970s with jokey film titles, like *Confessions of a Window Cleaner*, and nowadays 'confessions' usually means some kind of tawdry tale or revelation of sexual scandal.

Augustine, who wrote the original *Confessions* certainly had problems with sex and struggled with many issues, which are surprisingly modern, but in the book he was confessing his thoughts to God.

I wonder what your 'confessions to God' would look like – or mine?

Would we confess that we are lost? We somehow missed a turning, missed a great many turnings, and now find ourselves lost in brambles and thickets or, as the great Italian poet Dante described himself, 'lost in a dark wood'.

Psalm 23 is all about leading, guiding, finding our way back home… It is all about the Shepherd taking the initiative and leading us to good places, beyond our sorrows and confusions.

And in this great final verse, it is all about our destiny.

'I will dwell in the house of the Lord forever.'

The pain of longing to go home…

The Hebrew word which is translated as 'dwell' really means 'return'. I will return to the house of the Lord.

I love this beautiful and simple truth: we need to return.

We need to find our way back to where we truly belong, where we have always belonged. This is not just about finding our way to some place of divine peace, and it is not just about the idea of an afterlife – of one day finding ourselves in the presence of the

Shepherd Himself. All this is implied and, I believe, is a glorious reality.

But this verse is really about 'now'.

Now is the time to dwell in the house of the Lord. Now is the time to return.

The great spiritual writer Henri Nouwen says that the first love in our life is the love of God. All other loves are secondary, all human relationships, all longings and desires can only be seen in the light of this first love: 'First love is claiming again and again and again the truth of myself. And what is the truth of myself? That I am God's beloved child, long before I was born and my father and mother and my teachers and my church got involved, and I will be God's beloved child long after I've died. I go from God's intimate embrace to God's intimate embrace.'

The trouble with some religious traditions, and the trouble with our own experience of dysfunctional families or harsh and unsympathetic teachers, is that we grow up believing that we are essentially bad or unworthy of love, doomed to fail, to be excluded… and, at some deep level, we come to believe that our destiny is to be excluded from the house of the Lord. 'All that spiritual stuff is for good people. It's not for me.'

It is for you.

It is right here, in Psalm 23. It is your invitation card. It is your hand-written 'welcome home' card.

'I will dwell in the house of the Lord forever.'

The house speaks of safety and of identity. Many people long to have their own houses on earth and sadly many people will never have such a place. But this song ends with the greatest truth: you will always have a home in the love of God. Always.

We love to decorate our houses, those of us lucky enough to have such material security. We fill them with paintings and furniture that mean something special to us. We have cards on the shelves, or mementoes: a gift from a friend, a pebble from the shore, some books, perhaps, a prize we won at school (not in my case - my brother won all the cups). We create a haven of identity. It is our home, our refuge.

But everyone knows how fragile such human homes are. I have lived through a flood destroying everything in my house. I have been through the complete loss of a home and the division of all the possessions, because of a broken marriage. Last year, my cousin's home burned down and she lost everything. A few years ago, I talked to an African bishop whose home, containing all his recent wedding presents, was set on fire by terrorists. I asked him what he thought when he was standing in those terrible ruins. 'A verse from the Bible came to me,' he replied, '"A person's life does not consist in the abundance of the things he possesses"' (Luke 12.15). I was very moved by his courage and also by the sheer clarity of his vision.

It is quite true. Nothing is stable on earth. Not a beautiful house, not even the strongest and most beautiful and faithful marriage. Two years ago, my greatest female friend of 45 years, Miranda Harris, was killed in a terrible car accident. Last year, I spent time with her husband Peter, in the beautiful home which she created so lovingly and with such rare artistry. Every room was fragrant with her presence.

But she is not there. She is now – and her brave husband is the first to say so – 'in the house of the Lord forever'.

Our lives, our homes, our families, our careers, all the things that matter so much to us on earth, are temporary expressions of the deepest truth.

There is a home for us. There is a haven for us, which no one can ever take away. I will dwell in the house of the Lord forever.

Even the temple, which King David longed for so much and which was built in great splendour by his son Solomon, only lasted a few hundred years. It was destroyed by war. The temple was rebuilt only to be destroyed again. And finally, Herod built a massive temple which was reduced to rubble by the Romans in AD 70.

Temples ruined, houses destroyed, whole civilisations buried under shifting sands.

Do we think our own homes and our Western civilisation are somehow an exception to this fragility? Or that our lives on earth will be free from trouble and disaster? Do we think we can take a shortcut around the valley of the shadow of death? Perhaps miss out on death altogether, with the advance of science and artificial intelligence?

When we stop to think, we know that there is no safe place on earth and no opt-out clause from being human and mortal.

Henri Nouwen continues: 'You see, what God your Father in heaven said about you is this: "I'm sending you into this world for a little time, twenty, thirty, forty, sixty, seventy, eighty years, that's just a little bit, so that you have the chance to say: 'I love you too.'" Because life is simply saying yes to God as he says, over and over, "I love you."'

'I will dwell in the house of the Lord forever.'

I will return to the house of the Lord, where I have always belonged, where I come from, where I am going to, where my identity is secure, where I know that I am God's beloved and He is mine.

Dwelling in this place begins now. It is a daily calling, from when we wake up to when we go to bed. We are to live with Him through every moment of the day, in the most beautiful love relationship imaginable.

We are to sing the most beautiful song in the world every day.

Our whole lives, whatever is happening, good or bad, in friendship and in loneliness, in loving harmony or in agonising separation, in perfect fitness and in chronic ill-health: our whole lives are to be lived to the full, brimful, overflowing with the knowledge of God's intimate love for us. And each day of this life on earth will also be a dress rehearsal.

We will become familiar with a loving presence, with the truth at the heart of the universe. We will answer, in the deepest place of our own soul, Einstein's question: 'Is the universe a friendly place?'

We will say, 'Yes'.

We will live out this truth in all circumstances and sometimes against extreme odds, when life throws the most terrible shocks and contradictions at us.

Gradually, as we emerge from tragedy or despair, we will still say, quietly at first, 'Yes. Despite everything, I know this. I know that the universe is a friendly place. Because I know that I am God's beloved child.'

And as we live our lives like this, daily preparing, daily rehearsing, it will not be a surprise to us when, finally, we do enter God's presence for all eternity.

I sometimes think that, for many people, there must be a long period of adjustment following their arrival in the afterlife. 'So, it *is* true after all!' And, poignantly, 'Why did I waste my life on earth so stupidly pursuing empty dreams?'

But for those who have been preparing, who have been singing the most beautiful song, increasingly with every fibre of their being, it will surely be: 'Welcome! Everything is prepared for you. For you have been building this glorious home all your life and now you are ready to walk through the door.'

'I will dwell in the house of the Lord forever.'

Epilogue

So that's it. One hundred and eighteen words long. A poem which can be read in one minute. A song which can be sung in two minutes.

The most beautiful song in the world which can be sung as an anthem for a lifetime.

You may say, and I wouldn't blame you, 'This is all very well, so many fine sentiments and interesting observations, but how on earth do you "sing this song"? How do you live this psalm for a whole lifetime?'

The truth is: there are as many ways as there are people.

But let's start with some examples from different walks of life.

If you want to be physically fit, then you need to take some exercise every day. And you need to follow a good diet. You need discipline and routine.

The same is true if you want to be spiritually fit.

If you want to 'sing the most beautiful song in the world', you need to read this psalm often. I believe you need to learn it by heart. You need to make a habit of saying it to yourself in many different circumstances, for example, when you are lying in bed awake because you are worried.

It is very important to repeat the psalm in all circumstances, so it becomes second nature. It must become part of your 'good diet'. To say this psalm, quietly to yourself, is part of your exercise routine and you need to do this at times when you feel nothing and when you think it means nothing to you.

You need discipline and routine. This means, in my view, deciding to recite this psalm every day, perhaps in the morning when you get up and at night, before you go to sleep.

As I say, there are as many ways as there are people to sing this song for a lifetime. You need to find your own particular way.

Here's another image: if you are learning a language or studying for an A Level or a degree, you may well put Post-it Notes on your fridge, on the bathroom mirror, on the kitchen noticeboard, with quotes you need to learn or facts you need to absorb.

Why not concentrate for some days on a single line of the psalm, just like in this book? One line can be enough food for thought, enough nourishment to your spirit, for quite a while. You can put the psalm on Post-it Notes around your house.

You will find that new thoughts come to you about a single word or a line – no doubt ideas and feelings which I have not even mentioned in this book. Because it is personal.

'The Lord is my shepherd.'

We are not used to reading in this way. Hundreds of years ago, medieval monks and nuns talked of 'Lectio Divina', a form of 'divine reading'. This means not rushing through everything, which is how we often read.

We can read a novel with excitement, turning the pages eagerly. We can read a newspaper casually and quickly, skipping articles that do not interest us. We can skim the pages of a professional report that is rather dull to us – and try to 'get the gist' of it.

But this is not the way to read the psalm, any more than it is the way to eat a five-star meal cooked by a master chef.

We need to eat such a meal slowly, savouring the tastes, enjoying the rare combinations of food and spices and sauces... sipping vintage wine, relishing it on the palette.

As someone who has always eaten too fast (a fault I developed at boarding school, because if you didn't eat quickly, you missed a second helping), I have a great deal to learn about eating slowly and thoughtfully. I have also had to learn a great deal about reading slowly. I am a writer and I often have to read many books for research, and I have developed the skills to read extremely fast.

This is something I have to 'unlearn' when it comes to Psalm 23, or any of the Bible, for that matter.

Read slowly. Go back and read again. Consider what you have read. Allow it to settle. Quietly live with a word or a phrase or a single verse.

Return to the same passage again and again.

And begin to acquire the habit of praying and reading, for example: 'God help me to understand this.' Or, in the words of Psalm 119, 'Open my eyes, that I may see wonderful things in your law' (Psalm 119: 18). That is a great prayer. Wonderful things!

But it takes time, like looking for ancient treasure. It may take months or years to really discover deep meanings in familiar scriptures.

Don't be afraid of a new way of being, a new way of praying simply, or of reading with a truly open mind. What does Psalm 23 say to me today? In this tragic circumstance?

Everything depends on how determined we are, and we show this determination in many walks of life. For example, if we fall in love with someone and they don't reciprocate at first, we may well try to woo them, to gently persuade them, to convince them of our love with presents or kind gestures, beautiful handwritten cards…

In love, determination does not always pay off (although it often does), but in the spiritual realm it really does pay off.

Someone who wants to play the piano has to submit to hours, days, years of learning scales, of practising simple passages, of moving slowly and ambitiously towards harder and more profound pieces. It can take decades of patience and instruction.

I only made it to Grade 3, because I wasn't determined enough and I certainly wasn't ambitious enough at the age of nine. Too many distractions! Recently, a great friend died and bequeathed her grand piano to Freswick Castle, where I live – and I stare at this wonderful instrument and I wish I had kept going long enough with my piano lessons and exams to at least play a few tunes.

Thankfully, I can listen to wonderful musicians who visit, and I can admire their skill at the piano and appreciate their patience and determination.

Music and art and writing may be specific talents, which need nurturing and determination, but even these great art forms which can lift our spirits are not as important as the spiritual life itself.

And here is the good news. Everybody has the capacity to develop their spiritual life. It is not a question of talent or aptitude or being 'religious'. The word 'spiritual' comes from the Latin *spiritus*, which really means 'breath'. We may say, 'I'm not religious' meaning, 'I have no interest in church or all those rules and regulations and traditions.' But not many people say, 'I am not spiritual.' That would be like saying, 'I don't do much breathing.'

Spirituality is part of what it is to be human. So, to use another image, there is a 'level playing field' when it comes to spiritual training. We can all go into spiritual training and we can choose to do as much or as little as we want.

I believe that Psalm 23 is an ideal starting place and, even if that is all we ever read from the Bible (I hope not), it will have a profound effect on our life.

And not just on our lives, but on those around us.

Psalm 23, as it becomes part of our daily consciousness, can be embedded into our whole lives and our attitudes and our prayers. We can read and we can pray Psalm 23 for others.

If we have a friend in great need, we can quietly repeat the psalm in their favour, with their name: 'The Lord is Susan's shepherd, she shall not want... He makes her to lie down in green pastures.'

Of course, modern translations may well be

the best to use. A good and careful reader of this psalm may want to look at a number of different translations and constantly come at this beautiful song in many different ways.

'The Lord is my shepherd' has been set to music many times, and there are ancient and modern versions which we can learn to sing, as another aid on our journey.

Many years ago, I wrote a children's Bible (*The Lion Bible for Children*), and this is how I conveyed the psalm for young children:

The Lord is my shepherd, he gives me everything I need.
He lets me lie down in green meadows and
leads me beside peaceful streams.
He gives new strength to my soul.
He guides me in the way of goodness.
Even if I walk through nightmares and terrors,
down into the darkest valley of pain and death,
you are still there beside me; your arms comfort me,
your shepherd's crook protects me.
You have prepared wonderful things for me,
a joyful feast, even though my enemies surround me.
You anoint my head with oil;
my cup of happiness is so full, it is brimming over.
Goodness and mercy will follow me all the days of my life.
I will make my home in the house of the Lord my God,
forever and ever.

Find the translation that suits you best and learn that one. I still think that the Authorised Version is the finest! But a modernised version of the old one, which simply turns 'maketh' into 'makes' and so on, may be the best (and that is the one I have used throughout this book: the NKJV)

Let me end with the opening verse, in my children's version: 'The Lord is my shepherd; he gives me everything I need.' In your daily quest to 'sing the most beautiful song in the world', He will surely give you everything you need.

After all, He knows you best. He made you. And He loves you, far more than you will ever know or can ever discover, even by singing 'the most beautiful song in the world'.

Psalm 23

The Lord is my shepherd;
I shall not want.
He makes me to lie down in green pastures;
He leads me beside the still waters.
He restores my soul;
He leads me in the paths of righteousness
    for His name's sake.
Yea, though I walk through the valley
    of the shadow of death,
I will fear no evil, for You are with me;
Your rod and Your staff, they comfort me.
You prepare a table before me in the
    presence of my enemies;
You anoint my head with oil;
My cup overflows.
Surely goodness and mercy shall follow me
    all the days of my life;
And I will dwell in the house of the Lord forever.

Acknowledgements

I would like to thank my agent and friend, Tony Collins, for believing in this book so deeply and for taking it to the wonderful team at Waverly Abbey Trust. I am so grateful for their enthusiasm, encouragement and dedication.

There has never been a greater need for vision and strong hope for our world

The arts and media are at the forefront of our culture and The Wayfarer Trust seeks to bring creative and spiritual inspiration to artists of every kind.

The Trust provides an environment of hospitality and renewal at Freswick Castle, bringing people together from across the world. In recent years, our activities have included arts conferences, creative retreats and courses, projects with school children, inspirational books and videos and financial and moral support to artists and creative organisations

Although there is a special love and concern for artists, The Wayfarer Trust extends a warm welcome to people from every walk of life.

The Wayfarer Trust was founded 25 years ago by Murray Watts and continues to develop every year. Our vision is to create an ecology of hope in the lives of many – where creative innovation and abundant life can flourish for the future.

THE WAYFARER TRUST
FRESWICK CASTLE, WICK, CAITHNESS
SCOTLAND KW1 4XX

Scottish Charity No: SCO27212

info@wayfarertrust.org // www.wayfarertrust.org

Learn to be the Difference

Equipping people to be the positive impact on society through:

·   Nurturing personal growth;

·   Delivering academic excellence; and

·   Developing pastoral compassion

Courses and resources that equip you to be the difference where you are.